Save the Planet

Let's Recycle

Claire Llewellyn

Chrysalis Education

US publication copyright © 2003 Chrysalis Education.

International copyright reserved in all countries. No part of this book may be reproduced in any form without written permission from the publisher.

Distributed in the United States by
Smart Apple Media
1980 Lookout Drive
North Mankato, MN 56003

Copyright © Chrysalis Books PLC 2003

ISBN 1-93233-322-3

The Library of Congress control number 2003102557

Editorial Manager: Joyce Bentley
Senior Editor: Sarah Nunn
Design: Stonecastle Graphics Ltd
Illustrations: Paul B. Davies
Picture researcher: Paul Turner

Printed in China

10 9 8 7 6 5 4 3 2 1

Contents

What is recycling?

Recycling means using old **materials** to make new things. For example, it means using the paper in old magazines to make new paper tissues, notepads, and bags.

These towels have been made from recycled paper. ▼

The paper in old newspapers and cardboard cartons can be turned into new paper goods. This is an example of recycling.

▲
Recycling
means using
the glass in
old jars to
make brand
new bottles.

◄
Garden waste
and fruit and
vegetable
peelings can
be recycled
into **compost**.

What a waste!

Every week, we throw a lot of things away. Most of this garbage is made of useful materials, which could be recycled.

When our trash is taken away, valuable materials, such as metal and glass, are lost for ever.

Stop! The glass in this jar could be recycled. Throwing it away is a waste.

This is what we throw away
every week. Is it really garbage?

Glass bottles
and jars.

Rags and
old clothes.

Metal cans
and foil.

Plastic
bottles
and cartons.

Newspapers,
leaflets, old
envelopes,
old cards,
and food
packaging.

Food scraps,
vegetable
peelings, dead
flowers, and
other **organic
waste**.

Where does our trash go?

Most of our garbage is dumped in huge holes in the ground called **landfill sites**. There, it slowly begins to rot. This produces nasty **gases** and poisonous **liquids**, which trickle into the water supply deep underground.

Landfill sites are dirty and spoil the **environment**. We will not need so many of them if we throw less garbage away.

Some trash is burned in **incinerators**. This makes smoke that **pollutes** the air, and is harmful for us to breathe.

Getting rid of garbage

Most of us don't want to think about our garbage, we just want it to disappear. Look carefully at the picture below. Can you see why our trash cans are so full? What is being thrown away?

Every trash can is full up. This family has so much garbage, it has filled an extra bag!

These old newspapers are going in the trash can. They contain useful paper.

There is lots of useful metal in these cans but they are being thrown out too.

Empty glass bottles are being thrown away. They contain useful glass.

These "old" clothes don't fit any more, but they look as good as new.

These vegetable peelings could be made into compost for the garden.

A better way with garbage

There are other ways of getting rid of garbage without throwing it in the trash can. Can you see what they are in this picture? If every trash can was as empty as these, we would need fewer landfill sites.

The garbage is being sorted before it goes into the trash can.

Organic waste goes into the compost bin.

Everything made of paper is put in this box.

All the glass is put in this box.

Everything that can be recycled is taken to nearby **recycling points**.

There is very little garbage in the can.

Old clothes are given to charity shops.

All the cans go in this box.

13

Gathering raw materials

All the goods we buy and which, in time, we throw away are made from wood, metal, rock, oil, and other **raw materials**. These are hard to gather. It takes a lot of hard work, powerful machines, and a huge amount of **fuel**.

Paper is made from trees. The trees are cut down, put onto trucks, and driven along roads to paper mills.

▲ Rocks and minerals are the materials from which we make glass and many metals. It takes lots of **energy** to dig them out of the ground.

Digging, chopping, and building ▶ work spoils the environment. It destroys the **habitats** of animals and plants.

Using raw materials

Wood, rocks, and oil are taken to factories. Here, more machines get to work on them, changing them into useful materials such as paper, glass, and plastic. This takes a lot of energy, which comes from burning fuel.

Sand and rock have to be crushed and then heated to make glass.

Wooden logs have to be chopped up and soaked in water before they can be made into paper.

Fuels forever?
Factories burn coal, gas, and oil to get energy for their machines. These fuels won't last forever. We need to use them carefully.

Factories burn huge amounts of fuel. This makes smoke that pollutes the air.

Don't throw away–recycle!

When we throw something away, we waste the material and energy that were used to make it. Recycling is so much better. Recycling saves energy and takes fewer raw materials from the Earth.

Recycling glass is much easier than making it from raw materials. First, glass bottles are sorted, cleaned, and crushed.

Next, the crushed glass is heated till it melts. This takes a lot less energy than melting sand and rock!

Then the hot glass is shaped
into new bottles and jars.

Old trash, new materials

Just as glass can be recycled, so can paper, **aluminum**, steel, and some plastics. It takes far less energy to recycle these materials than to make them from scratch.

Old paper is chopped up and added to water to make new recycled paper.

Aluminum cans are crushed and heated to make new sheets of aluminum.

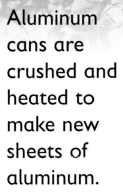

Plastic is not very easy to recycle, but some kinds can be used to make flower pots, furniture, traffic cones, and even fleece jackets.

Going shopping

Some of the goods we buy in the stores waste energy and raw materials. Have a look at the picture below. Can you see how careless shopping adds to the trash in our bins?

These plastic bottles are very small. They will not last long.

This fruit has a lot of packaging. It will all end up in the landfill.

Plastic bottles and other containers are usually thrown away when they are finished.

The paper in these tissues has been made from wood.

This shopper has lots of thin plastic bags. They will end up as garbage.

A better way of shopping

A wise shopper can cut down on waste. Look at the picture below. Can you see how people are saving energy and materials? This will mean less trash in their trash can!

This big plastic bottle will last for years. Refills come in paper cartons, which cuts out the need for extra plastic.

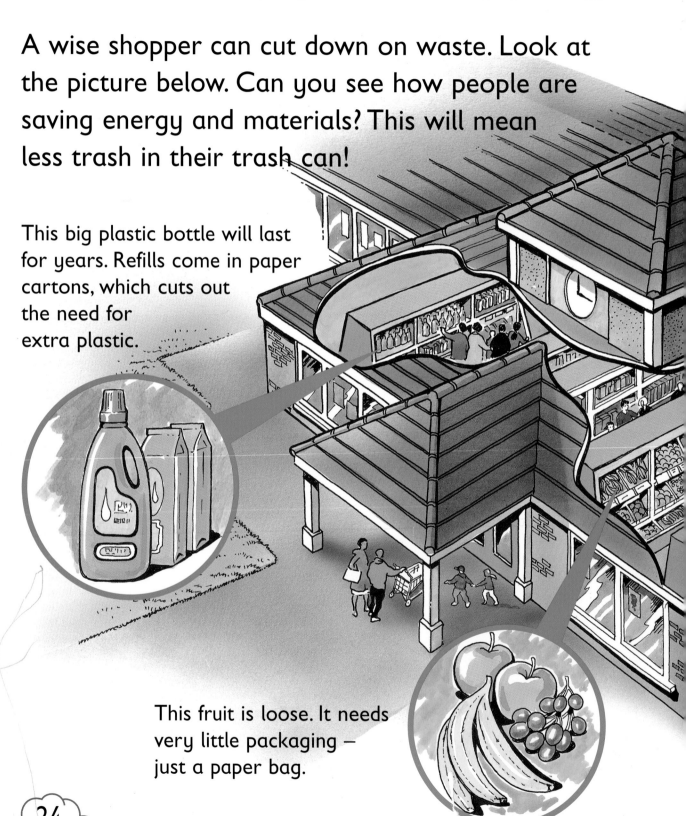

This fruit is loose. It needs very little packaging — just a paper bag.

These tissues are made from recycled paper. This uses less energy than tissues made from wood.

This shopping bag is very strong. It can be used over and over again.

These bottles are made of recycled glass. Glass is a better choice than plastic because it is easier to recycle.

Always look for this sign on the goods you buy. It shows they are made from recyclable materials.

Small steps, big results

Recycling your trash is a small step, so will it make a difference? Of course, it will! If your step is copied by millions of other people, the results for the Earth will be huge! Everyone shares the planet. Everyone can help to save it.

What would happen if everyone recycled their trash?

If everyone was good at recycling we wouldn't have so much trash to get rid of. There would be fewer incinerators and landfill sites. This would be good for the environment.

We would use fewer raw materials. This would save energy and protect wildlife habitats.

Factories would produce more recycled goods. This would save energy and cut the air pollution that comes from burning fuel.

Over to you!

Some places have laws to make people recycle. Other places do not. No one wants to see mountains of trash. Why not try one of the ideas below, and help to get people recycling?

Make posters to encourage people to recycle their trash. Think of a clever slogan like "Slim your bin!", "Think trash" or "Waste wise." Stick a poster on your trash bin or in your home, school, or library.

For one week, keep a record of everything that your family throws away. Highlight things that could have been recycled. Pin up your record for everyone to see.

Suggest that your parents have different containers for paper, glass, metal, and plastics, and offer to sort the trash.

Have you got room for a compost bin? Use it to store organic waste and in a few months you'll have compost to put on all your plants.

Do a survey to find out how many people in your class or school regularly recycle their trash.

Are there plenty of recycling points in your town? Are there any at your school? If not, complain! Write to your paper or talk to your teacher.

Does your school use recycled paper? If not, try and make them change their mind.

With a grown-up, sort out your old clothes, toys, and books and give them to friends, charity shops, or rummage sales.

Join a group that helps to protect the environment. Two of the groups you could try are:
Friends of the the Earth www.foei.org
Greenpeace www.greenpeace.org

Glossary

Aluminum A gray metal that is very light. It is used to make foil, cans, and many other things.

Compost The crumbly mixture we add to soil to help plants to grow. Compost is decayed organic waste.

Energy The power that makes machines and living things able to work. We can get energy from burning fuels.

Environment The land, air, and sea that make up the world around us.

Fuel Wood, coal, oil, or some other material that can be burned for heat and power.

Gas A substance like air that is not solid or liquid. Air is a mixture of different gases.

Habitat The natural home of an animal or plant.

Incinerator A machine that is used to burn unwanted things.

Landfill site A huge hole in the ground where trash is buried.

Liquid A substance like water that runs and flows.

Material Something like wood, metal, plastic, or glass that is used to make different things.

Organic waste Any waste, such as dead flowers or vegetable peelings, that is natural and comes from plants.

Packaging The wrapping that is used to pack foods and other things we buy.

Pollute To spoil the air, land, or water with harmful substances.

Raw material A natural material that is the starting point for making something new. Oil is the raw material that is used to make plastic.

Recycle To take an old material and use it again to make something new.

Recycling point A place where recyclable materials can be taken and deposited, ready for collection.

Index